International Labour and Employment Compliance Handbook

www.kluwerlawonline.com

Labour and Employment Compliance in Brazil

International Bar Association

Labour and Employment Compliance in Brazil

Fifth Edition

Rodrigo Seizo Takano
Andrea Giamondo Massei Rossi
Murilo Caldeira Germiniani

This publication is part of the International Labour and Employment Compliance Handbook, available on www.kluwerlawonline.com

Editors: Salvador del Rey and Robert J. Mignin

the global voice of the legal profession

Wolters Kluwer

Published by:
Kluwer Law International B.V.
PO Box 316
2400 AH Alphen aan den Rijn
The Netherlands
E-mail: international-sales@wolterskluwer.com
Website: lrus.wolterskluwer.com

Sold and distributed in North, Central and South America by:
Wolters Kluwer Legal & Regulatory U.S.
7201 McKinney Circle
Frederick, MD 21704
United States of America
Email: customer.service@wolterskluwer.com

Sold and distributed in all other countries by:
Air Business Subscriptions
Rockwood House
Haywards Heath
West Sussex
RH16 3DH
United Kingdom
Email: international-customerservice@wolterskluwer.com

ISBN 978-94-035-0390-5

e-Book: ISBN 978-94-035-0391-2
web-PDF: ISBN 978-94-035-0392-9

All listed titles are also available on lrus.wolterskluwer.com

1. Argentina: Julio César Stefanoni Zani & Enrique Alfredo Betemps, *Labour and Employment Compliance in Argentina, 6th edition*, 2018 (ISBN 978-94-035-0373-8)
2. Australia: John Tuck, Stephen Price, Rosemary Roach, Jack de Flamingh, Nicholas Ellery & Nick Le Mare, *Labour and Employment Compliance in Australia, 3rd edition*, 2018 (ISBN 978-94-035-0380-6)
3. Belgium: Chris Van Olmen, *Labour and Employment Compliance in Belgium, 3rd edition*, 2018 (ISBN 978-94-035-0383-7)
4. Brazil: Rodrigo Seizo Takano, Andrea Giamondo Massei Rossi & Murilo Caldeira Germiniani, *Labour and Employment Compliance in Brazil, 5th edition*, 2018 (ISBN 978-94-035-0390-5)
5. Canada: Kevin Coon & Adrian Ishak, *Labour and Employment Compliance in Canada, 2nd edition*, 2014 (ISBN 978-90-411-5637-2)
6. Chile: Gerardo Otero A., Maria Dolores Echeverria F., Macarena López M. & María de los Ángeles Fernández S., *Labour and Employment Compliance in Chile, 6th edition*, 2018 (ISBN 978-94-035-0393-6)
7. China: King & Wood Mallesons, *Labour and Employment Compliance in China, 5th edition*, 2018 (ISBN 978-94-035-0400-1)
8. England: Tony Hyams-Parish, *Labour and Employment Compliance in England, 6th edition*, 2018 (ISBN 978-94-035-0403-2)
9. France: Pascale Lagesse, *Labour and Employment Compliance in France, 6th edition*, 2018 (ISBN 978-94-035-0410-0)
10. Germany: Gerlind Wisskirchen & Martin Lützeler, *Labour and Employment Compliance in Germany, 6th edition*, 2018 (ISBN 978-94-035-0413-1)
11. India: Manishi Pathak, *Labour and Employment Compliance in India, 6th edition*, 2018 (ISBN 978-94-035-0420-9)
12. Ireland: Duncan Inverarity & Sinéad Grace, *Labour and Employment Compliance in Ireland, 5th edition*, 2018 (ISBN 978-94-035-0423-0)
13. Israel: Yaron Horovitz, Pnina Broder-Manor & Helen Raziel, *Labour and Employment Compliance in Israel, 5th edition*, 2018 (ISBN 978-94-035-0430-8)
14. Italy: Angelo Zambelli, *Labour and Employment Compliance in Italy, 6th edition*, 2018 (ISBN 978-94-035-0433-9)
15. Japan: Yoshikazu Sugino, *Labour and Employment Compliance in Japan, 6th edition*, 2018 (ISBN 978-94-035-0440-7)
16. Republic of Korea: Sang Wook Cho, Soojung Lee & Christopher Mandel, *Labour and Employment Compliance in the Republic of Korea, 4th edition*, 2018 (ISBN 978-94-035-0453-7)
17. Mexico: Oscar De La Vega Gómez, *Labour and Employment Compliance in Mexico, 6th edition*, 2018 (ISBN 978-94-035-0443-8)
18. The Netherlands: Els de Wind & Cara Pronk, *Labour and Employment Compliance in the Netherlands, 4th edition*, 2018 (ISBN 978-94-035-0470-4)
19. Poland: Barbara Jóźwik, *Labour and Employment Compliance in Poland, 6th edition*, 2018 (ISBN 978-94-035-0450-6)

20. Russia: Anna-Stefaniya Chepik, *Labour and Employment Compliance in Russia*, 2013 (ISBN 978-90-411-4925-1)
21. Saudi Arabia: Sara Khoja & Sarit Thomas, *Labour and Employment Compliance in Saudi Arabia, 1st edition,* 2018 (ISBN 978-94-035-0490-2)
22. South Africa: Susan Stelzner, Stuart Harrison, Brian Patterson & Zahida Ebrahim, *Labour and Employment Compliance in South Africa, 6th edition*, 2018 (ISBN 978-94-035-0460-5)
23. Spain: Salvador del Rey & Ana Campos, *Labour and Employment Compliance in Spain, 6th edition*, 2018 (978-94-035-0463-6)
24. Turkey: Sertaç Kökenek & Elif Nur Çakır, *Labour and Employment Compliance in Turkey, 4th edition*, 2018 (ISBN 978-94-035-0473-5)
25. United Arab Emirates: Sara Khoja & Sarit Thomas, *Labour and Employment Compliance in the United Arab Emirates, 5th edition*, 2018 (ISBN 978-94-035-0480-3)
26. United States: Baker & McKenzie LLP, *Labour and Employment Compliance in the United States, 4th edition*, 2018 (ISBN 978-94-035-0483-4)

International Bar Association
The Global Voice of the Legal Profession

The International Bar Association (IBA), established in 1947, is the world's leading organization of international legal practitioners, bar associations and law societies. The IBA influences the development of international law reform and shapes the future of the legal profession throughout the world. It has a membership of over 40,000 individual lawyers and almost 200 bar associations and law societies spanning all continents. It has considerable expertise in providing assistance to the global legal community.

Grouped into two divisions – the Legal Practice Division and the Public and Professional Interest Division – the IBA covers all practice areas and professional interests, providing members with access to leading experts and up-to-date information. Through the various committees of the divisions, the IBA enables an interchange of information and views among its members as to laws, practices and professional responsibilities relating to the practice of business law around the globe. Additionally, the IBA's high-quality publications and world-class conferences provide unrivalled professional development and network-building opportunities for international legal practitioners and professional associates.

The IBA's Bar Issues Commission provides an invaluable forum for IBA member organisations to discuss all matters relating to law at an international level.

The IBA's Human Rights Institute (IBAHRI) works across the Association, to promote, protect and enforce human rights under a just rule of law, and to preserve the independence of the judiciary and the legal profession worldwide.

Other institutions established by the IBA include the Southern Africa Litigation Centre and the International Legal Assistance Consortium.

Employment and Industrial Relations Law Committee

The aims of the committee are to develop and exchange knowledge of employment and industrial relations law and practice. Members support each other through the provision of innovative ideas and practical assistance on day-to-day issues. In addition, through its journal and through presentations, conferences, the committee ensures the dissemination of up-to-date law and practice in this highly important business area.

International Bar Association Global Employment Institute

The IBA Global Employment Institute (IBA GEI) was formed in early 2010 for the purpose of developing for multinationals and worldwide institutions a global and strategic approach to the key legal issues in the human resources and human capital fields.

Drawing on the resources and expertise of the IBA membership, the IBA GEI will provide a unique contribution in the field of employment, discrimination and immigration law, on a diverse range of global issues, to private and public organizations throughout the world. The IBA GEI is designed to enhance the management, performance and productivity of these organizations and help achieve best practice in their human capital and management functions from a strategic perspective.

The IBA GEI will become the leading voice and authority on global HR issues by virtue of having a number of the world's leading labour and employment practitioners in its ranks, and the support and resource of the world's largest association of international lawyers.

Further information

International Bar Association, 4th Floor, 10 St Bride Street, London EC4A 4AD, United Kingdom, Tel: +44 (0)20 7842 0090, Fax: +44 (0)20 7842 0091, E-mail: member@int-bar.org, www.ibanet.org

About the International Labour and Employment Compliance Handbook

From 1976 through 1988, the International Bar Association and Kluwer Law International published the groundbreaking International Handbook on Contracts of Employment. This Handbook provided one of the first global overviews of the law of the international employment relationship.

Since publishing the first edition, globalization of business has created an increased demand for knowledge of labor and employment laws throughout the world. Therefore, along with Kluwer, we decided to publish an updated Handbook which we have titled the International Labour and Employment Compliance Handbook.

This new Handbook was intended to be a practical guide by providing a general overview of key labor and employment issues in multiple jurisdictions. Each chapter was written so that it is easy to understand by lawyers and non-lawyers alike. Each country author has also followed a standard outline to assist readers in analysing employment issues in each country.

The first edition of this new Handbook included nineteen (19) different countries.

This Handbook would not have been possible without the help and assistance of many people. Most importantly, the individual country authors are all distinguished legal practitioners who spent considerable time drafting and revising their country reports to meet difficult deadlines. We thank each of them. Our friends at Kluwer, especially Ewa Szkatula, have done a wonderful job in keeping the editors and the authors on schedule. Finally, we want to also express our gratitude to Cuatrecasas, Gonçalves Pereira, and Baker & McKenzie LLP for their valuable assistance in the coordination and organization of this project. Our warmest thanks to each of them.

Because of the success of the Handbook,Wolters Kluwer Law & Business decided to publish each country report also as a separate book to give a choice in obtaining the information. We hope this new format will be a helpful and useful resource just like the Handbook. Both formats are available in print and online.

The Editors

Salvador del Rey Guanter
Robert J. Mignin

March 2013

Legal Compliance in Brazil

Legal Compliance in Brazil

1. LEGAL FRAMEWORK: EMPLOYMENT LAWS

In Brazil, employment and labor relations are governed mainly by the Brazilian Federal Constitution, the Brazilian Labor Law (*Consolidação das Leis do Trabalho*—CLT), Brazilian social security laws and regulations, normative rules and regulations issued by the Brazilian Labor and Employment Ministry, other specific employment- and labor-related laws (hereinafter collectively referred to as "Brazilian employment and labor laws") and collective bargaining agreements.

Brazilian Federal Constitution establishes fundamental labor and employment rights for rural and urban employees. In particular, its Article 7 lists the basic labor and employment rights that must be guaranteed to employees. Among such basic rights, there are, for example, protection against salary reduction and discrimination due to gender, age, race and marital status.

Brazilian Labor Law not only regulates the basic rights granted by the Brazilian Federal Constitution, but also encompasses a wide array of rights and obligations that must be observed by employees and employers during the term of the employment relationship and at its termination, such as the right to paid annual vacations plus an annual vacation bonus, working hours, overtime premium, maternity and paternity leaves, mandatory severance payments, meal breaks, etc.

Also, Brazilian Labor Law governs the filing of labor lawsuits and administrative proceedings before Brazilian labor courts by employees, labor authorities and employers, and, together with the normative rules and regulations issued by the Brazilian Labor and Employment Ministry, addresses specific rules regarding health and safety in the workplace.

Brazilian Labor Law has been recently updated by Law No. 13,467/2017 (the so-called Labor and Employment Reform). The Labor and Employment

Reform implemented major changes to the Brazilian Labor Law as of November 11, 2017. Among of the main points of the Labor and Employment Reform, it can be highlighted: (a) the possibility of dividing vacations in up to three periods (one period of at least fourteen calendar days, being the other periods not less than five calendar days); (b) changes in equal pay for equal work rules; (c) new rules regarding working hours and offsetting of working hours; (d) new rules regarding home office; (e) new rules regarding part-time work; (f) changes in the rules regarding the collection of union dues due by employees; (g) new rules regarding termination of employment; (h) new rules regarding mutual agreement termination; (i) new rules regarding mass terminations; and (j) new rules regarding release agreements (company and employee may file a specific lawsuit before courts to ratify a release agreement and make it enforceable and binding to both parties).

In addition, on November 14, 2017, the Labor and Employment Reform was further amended by a Provisional Measure issued by President Michel Temer. The Provisional Measure amended a few controversial points of the Labor and Employment Reform. However, due to lack of political consensus in the Brazilian National Congress, the Provisional Measure was not approved by the Brazilian National Congress and, thus, the amendments included by the Provisional Measure lost their effectives as of April 23, 2018.

Due to this, as of April 23, 2018, the changes implemented by the Labor and Employment Reform are now in force as per its original text.

Collective bargaining agreements are the result of negotiations between labor unions representing employees and unions representing employers, or between a single employer and the labor union representing its employees. They aim at implementing specific employment conditions in addition to those foreseen by Brazilian employment and labor laws applicable only to the parties involved. In general, collective bargaining agreements establish rules regarding minimum salary applicable to the employees, annual salary increases, unhealthy and hazardous premiums, overtime premium, transportation allowance, meal tickets, etc. Although collective bargaining agreements have the same status as Brazilian employment and labor laws, they cannot reduce statutory rights protected by the Brazilian Federal Constitution and by the Brazilian Labor Law (specifically those described in Article 611—B, which was included by the Labor and Employment Reform). In addition to that, employers must comply with all of their provisions, under the penalty of the application of contractual and administrative fines and/or the filling of labor lawsuits requesting the compliance with it. Collective bargaining agreements usually remain in effect for twelve months.

Finally, there are also specific laws and regulations applicable to employment relationships, such as Law No. 4,090/1962, that regulates the payment of the annual 13th salary, Law No. 9,029/1995, that prohibits discrimination in the workplace and during hiring procedures, Law No. 8,036/1990, that regulates the deposits that must be carried out by employers into their employees' Severance Guarantee Fund, and other laws regulating specific professions, such as Decree-Law No. 972/1969, that regulates the hiring of journalists, and Law No. 7,377/1985, that regulates the hiring of secretaries.

2. CONTRACTS OF EMPLOYMENT

2.1. Overview

In order to hire an individual under an employment relationship, companies must registry the main terms and conditions of the employment (e.g., starting date, position and monthly salary) in the individual's Employment and Social Security Booklet (*Carteira de Trabalho e Previdência Social*—CTPS), under the penalty of being subject to administrative fines.

Although it is a common procedure adopted by most companies, the execution of a written employment agreement to govern the employment relationship is not required under Brazilian employment laws. In the absence of a written agreement, the relationship will be governed by Brazilian employment and labor laws, and the relevant collective bargaining agreement.

Generally, employment conditions previously established between the parties cannot be amended without the consent of the employee. In any case, amendments to employment conditions shall not worsen the employment conditions previously established between the parties in any way, even with the consent of the employee, under the penalty of being considered null and void.

2.2. Written Contracts of Employment

Contracts of employment may be open ended or executed for a fixed-term. In case the term is not specified in the contract, it will be considered as an open ended contract. Open ended contracts of employment, with a maximum ninety-day probation period, are the most common in Brazil.

As a general rule, fixed-term contracts of employment may only be established for a maximum period of two years and to regulate transient activities or jobs, meaning that they cannot regulate permanent tasks. Upon the expiration of the term established in the contract of employment, if it is not terminated, it will become an open ended contract of employment for all legal purposes.

Although a written contract of employment is not mandatory in Brazil, as the employment conditions registered in the employee's Employment and Social Security Booklet are very basic, it is highly recommendable to execute one in order to regulate additional employment conditions, such as working hours and voluntary benefits provided to the employee.

In addition to that, in accordance with the new rules implemented by the Labor and Employment Reform, employees who hold a higher education degree and receive a monthly salary equal to or greater than two times the maximum benefit paid by the National Social Security Institute (currently, this amount is equal to BRL 11,291.60[1]) may individually negotiate specific rules related to their employment contract. Among those, such employees may negotiate rules related to: (i) working hours; (ii) positions that are considered as position of trust for purposes of controlling working hours; (iii) home office, on call duty and intermittent work; (iv) alternative systems to control working hours; and (v) variable remuneration. Thus, especially for those employees, a written contract of employment is highly recommendable.

Moreover, for employees holding key positions, provisions related to confidentiality, nonsolicitation and noncompete obligations and proprietary rights must also be regulated by a written contract of employment.

2.3. Verbal Contracts of Employment

In the absence of a written contract of employment or of evidence concerning the conditions negotiated between the parties, it is presumed that the basic conditions provided for by Brazilian employment and labor laws are applicable. In this sense, it will be assumed that the employment relationship is open ended and that the employee was hired to work up to eight hours per day and forty-four hours per week (unless otherwise established by specific laws or the applicable collective bargaining agreement) and to hold a position consistent with his/her professional background.

In addition to that, based on the general principle of substance over form, employment conditions verbally negotiated may be enforceable before labor courts in case of a labor lawsuit if the interested party is able to evidence that such conditions were indeed verbally agreed.

1. This amount is valid for 2018 and may increase every year.

2.4. Intermittent Employment Agreement

The Labor and Employment Reform created a new type of employment agreement: the intermittent employment agreement.

Intermittent employees are subordinated to their respective employers, but work on a noncontinuous basis, in alternate periods, determined in hours, days, or months, regardless of the company's activity/business.

This type of employment agreement must be executed in writing and must set forth the hourly salary, which cannot be lower than the minimum hourly wage or than the hourly salary of other employees who work in the same position pursuant to an intermittent or regular employment agreement.

The employer shall call upon the employee at least three days in advance for the rendering of services. As of the moment the employee is called upon, the employee has to respond to the call. In case the employee does not respond, the employer may assume the employee's refusal. In addition to that, the period of inactivity of the employee shall not be considered as time available to the employer, and the employee may provide services to other employers.

Intermittent employees may have simultaneous intermittent employment contracts with other employers to complement their income.

At the end of each service period, the employee must immediately receive the following payments: (i) salary; (ii) proportional vacation, plus vacation bonus; (iii) proportional 13th salary; (iv) paid weekly rest; and (v) other mandatory legal allowances (if any). Every twelve months, employees acquire the right to enjoy, during the twelve subsequent months, one month's vacation, during which period he/she cannot work for the same employer.

2.5. Employee Handbook and Internal Policies

In Brazil, there is no specific law regulating employers' and employees' rights and obligations arising from internal policies, codes of conduct and/or employee handbooks.

Brazilian labor courts, however, recognize the employer's right to establish internal rules to assure the necessary protection and organization of its business, as well as a safe, healthy and fair work environment, provided that they do not conflict with the general rules and principles foreseen by Brazilian employment and labor laws. As an example, companies are allowed to establish internal policies regulating the monitoring of professional e-mails to protect business confidential information.

In addition to that, rights and benefits granted by companies through employee handbooks and/or internal policies are binding and, therefore, as a general rule, shall not be discontinued or modified unilaterally by the company if such modification is detrimental to the employees. In this sense, in order to legally amend internal policies concerning rights and benefits granted to employees, companies must, first, analyze potential impacts on employees' acquired rights.

On the other hand, policies concerning the company's internal organization may be easily amended.

2.6. Job Descriptions

In Brazil, job descriptions are not mandatory. However, if the employer chooses to have job descriptions, it is important that such description reflects the activities and responsibilities carried out by the employee in order to avoid potential claims based on equal pay for equal work rules.

2.7. Offer Letters

The terms and conditions of an offer letter are binding once the letter is delivered to a candidate. From the moment it is delivered, it has the same effect of a written contract of employment.

Usually, offer letters address only the basic and general conditions of the employment, such as position, base salary and benefits. Thus, in most of the cases, the conditions therein may be fully further addressed in a written contract of employment. It is important to clarify that, as a general rule, the contract of employment cannot supersede the offer letter, but solely complement it. In case both instruments conflict, the conditions more favorable to the employee will prevail.

3. RECRUITING, INTERVIEWING, SCREENING AND HIRING EMPLOYEES

3.1. Overview

As Brazilian employment and labor laws require the payment of mandatory severance for employees terminated without cause, employers shall deploy efficient ways to ensure the attraction and selection of the most suitable candidates in order to: (i) avoid losing potential talents; (ii) reduce turnover; and (iii) reduce severance-related costs. In addition to that, human resources and legal teams shall cooperate during hiring procedures to ensure that Brazilian employment and labor laws (especially the ones regarding discrimination) are being complied with.

3.2. Recruiting

There is no mandatory procedure to recruit employees, and each company may adopt its own recruiting process.

However, according to Brazilian Federal Constitution, Brazilian employment and labor laws and general principles of nondiscrimination, companies cannot limit the candidates' pool based on a discriminatory reason (e.g., based on gender or age), without a valid reason.

In addition to that, according to Brazilian employment and labor laws, companies cannot request from candidates evidences of past experience longer than six months.

3.3. Employment Applications

Companies must always ensure confidential treatment, protection and proper use of information obtained in application processes. This is so because, Article 5, item X, of Brazilian Federal Constitution protects the individual's privacy and intimacy. Please refer to item 25.

3.4. Pre-employment Inquiries

As a general rule, companies are free to establish their own recruiting procedures and pre-employment inquiries.

Nevertheless, companies cannot violate their candidates' intimacy, honor, private life and image. In this sense, general principles of law and Brazilian employment laws may restrict access to information that have no relevance and can lead to discrimination. For example, according to Law No. 9,029/1995, companies cannot subject women to pregnancy tests.

In this sense, as a general rule, companies are authorized to conduct investigations into personal information of candidates provided that: (i) the information is obtained by legal means; (ii) the candidate is aware of the possibility of being investigated; (iii) the candidate expressly accepts the research; and (iv) the information obtained is not used in a discriminatory manner.

3.5. Pre-employment Tests and Examinations

Pre-employment tests and examinations may be performed to the extent that they are necessary to assess the employees' capabilities for the position.

Examinations unrelated to employees' activities may be deemed as violations to the candidate's private life and may not be legal.

3.5.1. Blood Tests

In order to avoid labor-related claims based on discrimination, it is highly recommendable for companies intending to submit candidates to blood tests to detect drugs and alcohol use/abuse to: (a) ensure the existence of an effective connection between the tests and the activities that will be carried out by the candidate once he/she is hired; (b) obtain full consent of the candidate for the tests, without any kind of coercion; and (c) perform the tests on nondiscriminatory manner (i.e., all candidates for the relevant position should be subject to the test, irrespective of other personal characteristics).

3.5.2. Reference Checks

As there are no legal provisions prohibiting companies to request candidates to provide references from their prior employers, companies are free to request and verify the accuracy of all information provided by candidates, such as academic credentials, professional experience, expertise, etc.

3.5.3. Credit Checks

Brazilian case law does not allow the denial of employment based on credit restrictions, even if the position is for a financial or accounting department. However, if the company is a financial institution authorized to operate by the Brazilian Central Bank, certain specific rules may apply.

3.5.4. Criminal Background Checks

Brazilian case law does not allow the denial of employment to candidates based on their criminal records. This rule, however, does not apply if statue or case law specifically establishes that, in order to hold a certain position, the employee cannot have criminal records (e.g., security guards).

Criminal background checks within recruiting procedures are also limited. According to the Superior Labor Court's understanding, the request of criminal records from candidates/employees would generate moral damages, except in the following cases: (a) when the request is expressly allowed by

Brazilian laws (e.g., security guards); (b) when the request is justified due to the nature of the work/position; and (c) when the request is justified due to the high level of trust required for the work/position (e.g., banking employees, employees who work with confidential information).

3.6. Interviewing

There are no legal provisions regulating job interviews. However, based on general principles of nondiscrimination, recruiters must avoid asking questions that may lead to discrimination. In this sense, for example, questions on sexual orientation and religious beliefs should be avoided.

3.7. Hiring Procedures

Companies must carry out the following procedures upon the hiring of an employee: (i) registering the employment information in the employee's Employment and Social Security Booklet; (ii) informing the hiring to the Brazilian Labor and Employment Ministry through specific forms that must be delivered by companies; (iii) subjecting the employee to a medical exam in order to confirm that he/she is fit for duty before the beginning of the activities; and (iv) registering the hiring in the Company's Registry Book.

3.8. Fines and Penalties

Companies that discriminate against candidates or conduct background checks or exams unrelated to the position may face: (i) investigations carried out by the Public Labor Prosecutor's Office that may lead to an administrative proceeding or even a class action claiming for the payment of compensation for collective damages; and/or (ii) labor lawsuits filed by candidates claiming for the payment of compensation for moral damages.

4. MANAGING PERFORMANCE/CONDUCT

4.1. Overview

Under Brazilian employment and labor laws, employees are subject to their employers' direction and powers of administration. Employers may also have to comply with internal disciplinary rules once they have been made public to their employees. Usually, the rules are presented to the employee on the hiring date, by means of an internal procedures and disciplinary rules handbook. Another common way to disclose such rules is by making them available at the company's intranet.

The performance appraisal is a process that helps to evaluate the excellence and the qualities of an employee, especially his/her contributions to the company and the development of its business. Moreover, it should also be used to inform the employee of his/her job performance. The performance appraisal may vary from company to company and, although there are no legal provisions regulating this matter in Brazil, most Brazilian companies adopt a performance appraisal. Smaller companies, however, usually adopt a more discretionary type of appraisal.

Considering that there is no legal provision regulating it, evaluations may have different perspectives, such as: (i) superiors evaluating their subordinates; (ii) co-workers evaluating co-workers; (iii) employees evaluating their superiors; and (iv) self-evaluations.

Employees under the performance evaluation of their superiors should be advised that the main purposes of the evaluation are to verify the achievement of the preestablished targets, to define future projections and targets and, in some cases, to justify promotions or payment of bonuses; and not to point out errors for the purposes of applying disciplinary measures. In the same sense, employees evaluating co-workers and their superiors should take into consideration ethics, the company's policies and should be free from any personal influences. Moreover, performance evaluations are important to provide a feedback to employees, to establish new goals and to improve performance.

4.2. Coaching and Counseling

There are no legal requirements for companies to provide counseling or coaching to their employees. Despite the lack of legal provisions in this regard, some companies have an internal policy for coaching and counseling. Their objective is to provide their employees with a better view of their job expectations and responsibilities, a feedback of their performance, and help them to improve any deficient skill in order to reach job expectations.

4.3. Written Evaluations

Companies that have internal policies to promote or compensate their employees (e.g., by increasing their salaries or paying bonuses) usually provide an annual (or more frequent) written evaluation based on previously established criteria that should have been previously disclosed to their employees. Generally, a copy of the written evaluation is given to the employees.

4.4. Warnings, Suspensions and Termination for Cause

To maintain order in the work environment, companies may apply disciplinary measures, always measured and based on a sense of justice, especially considering that Brazilian employment and labor laws protect employees from arbitrary acts of their employers. In this sense, companies are allowed to subject their employees to disciplinary measures ranging from a simple verbal warning up to the termination of employment for cause, according to the seriousness of the misconduct.

Warnings

A warning is a notice sent to an employee to give him/her knowledge of his/her misconduct, as well as the consequences in case of relapse. It may advise the employee that his/her employment will be terminated if his/her conduct does not change. It aims at describing the employee's behavior or actions, informing that such behavior or actions are unacceptable under law and the company's policies and that he/she must change his/her behavior or not repeat such action.

Warnings may be verbal or written. However, verbal warnings are only recommendable to small or less important wrongdoings. Written warnings are recommendable to prove that the employee was aware of his/her wrongdoing, especially in case of judicial questionings if such misconduct ends up in a termination for cause.

Some companies in Brazil apply, first, a verbal warning and, in case of relapse, a written one, depending on the seriousness of the misconduct of the employee. Since there are no legal requirements defining or specifying the applicable measures that employers should take, a warning may be applied based on predefined company's rules and common sense.

Suspensions

An employee should only be suspended in cases of severe misconduct. Employees are not paid during the suspension period. Regardless of the seriousness of the employee's misconduct, the suspension period cannot last more than thirty days. A longer suspension period may entitle the employee to terminate his/her employment for cause, case in which all severance payments due in case of termination without cause will be due to the employee.

Termination for Cause

In Brazil, employers may only terminate an employee for cause in the following hypotheses foreseen by Article 482 of Brazilian Labor Law: (a) dishonesty; (b) misconduct or bad behavior; (c) habitual engagement of the employee in commercial transactions on his/her own account or for another one without his/her employer's permission, if this involves competition with the undertaking in which he/she is employed or is prejudicial to the performance of his/her work; (d) a final decision issued by a criminal court, without the suspension of the execution of the penalty; (e) idleness of the employee in the performance of his/her duties; (f) habitual drunkenness or drunkenness while on duty;[2] (g) disclose of a secret of the undertaking; (h) breach of discipline or insubordination; (i) desertion of post; (j) any act detrimental to the honor or good image of another one committed during the employment, or an assault under the same conditions, except in case of legitimate self-defense or defense of another one; (k) any act detrimental to the honor or good reputation of, or an assault against the employer or a superior, except in case of legitimate self-defense or defense of another one; (l) habitual indulgence in games of chance; and (m) loss of qualification of the requirements established by law for the exercise of the employee's profession, as a result of a willful misconduct of the employee.

Terminations for cause will only be considered legal if the following requirements are present: (i) at least one of the hypothesis described above occurs (legal provision requirement); (ii) the termination is carried out as soon as the misconduct is verified by the employer (immediacy requirement), under the penalty of the conduct of the employer being considered as a tacit forgiveness; (iii) there is a direct relationship of cause and effect between the employee's offense and the employer's damages (connection requirement); and (iv) the punishment is proportional to employee's failure, meaning that his/her violation must be very serious, to the point that the trust of the employer on the employee is destroyed (proportionality requirement).

In this sense, in case the fourth requirement listed above is not met, the employer shall not terminate the employee for cause, but only: (i) apply any other penalty described above, according to the seriousness of the employee's offense; or (ii) terminate the employee without cause, upon the payment of all mandatory benefits and fines foreseen by Brazilian Labor Law.

---

2. Brazilian labor courts understand that alcoholism is an illness and alcohol consumption by addicts should no longer be used as a basis for disciplinary actions or termination for cause. That said, if the employer verifies that one of its employees is addicted to alcohol, he/she should not be punished or terminated for cause, but rather referred for treatment to the social security authorities.

5. TERMINATION OF EMPLOYMENT

5.1. Overview

According to Brazilian employment laws, an employment relationship may be terminated by companies: (i) without cause; or (ii) for cause.

On the other hand, employees may: (i) resign; or (ii) file a claim of constructive termination.

Finally, the parties may terminate the employment by mutual agreement.

Termination Without Cause by the Company

Employees may be terminated without cause at any time and at the entire discretion of the employer, as long as it complies with the relevant employment and labor laws and the applicable collective bargaining agreement, and carries out the payment of all mandatory severance charges due to the employee. Exception to the general rule relates to employees who are covered by any legal or statutory guarantee of employment.[3]

Employers may terminate an employment relationship without cause by giving a prior notice to employee of, at least, thirty days, up to ninety days, depending on how long the employment relationship has lasted. Such prior notice, however, may be paid in lieu by the employer if it intends to immediately terminate the employment relationship.

Employment agreements executed for a determined period may also be terminated prior to the term established between the parties provided that the relevant rules are complied with. In this case, specific rules may apply.

In case the employee is entitled to a guarantee of employment and the employer still intends to terminate him/her without cause, he/she will be entitled to receive an indemnification equal to the amounts that would have been paid to him/her during the outstanding guarantee of employment period. However, there are some guarantees of employment that, depending on the case, cannot be indemnified by the employer (e.g., the guarantee of

3. Guarantees of employment may be established by law or the relevant collective bargaining agreement. According to Brazilian employment and labor laws, employees are entitled to the following guarantee of employment: (a) pregnant employees: guarantee of employment begins as from the conception and ends five months after the delivery; (b) employees who are members of the Internal Committee for Accident Prevention: guarantee of employment begins as from the registration of the candidate and ends after the election or one year after the end of the mandate; (c) employees who suffered labor-related accidents or occupational diseases: guarantee of employment begins as from the date the employee returns to work and ends twelve months following such date; and (d) union representatives: guarantee of employment begins as from the registration of the candidate and ends after the election or one year after the end of the mandate.

employment to which the union representative is entitled). In these cases, if the employee is terminated without cause, he/she may file a labor lawsuit before the term of the guarantee of employment period claiming for his/her reinstatement to his/her previous position.

Termination for Cause by the Company

Terminations for cause by the employer may solely take place in the hypotheses foreseen by Article 482 of Brazilian Labor Law. Please refer to item 4.4.

Resignation by the Employee

Employees may resign at any time, at their own discretion, without cause.

Constructive Termination

In some cases, the employee may file a claim of constructive termination.

A constructive termination may be declared by courts whenever the employer commits a serious misconduct, as established in Article 483 of the Brazilian Labor Law. A serious misconduct may be characterized when: (i) the employer demands from their employees services that are superior than their strength, prohibited by law, contrary to good customs or unrelated to the contract; (ii) employees are treated with excessive strictness by the employer or their superiors; (iii) employees are in eminent danger of considerable harm; (iv) employer fails to comply with the obligations established in the employment contract; (v) employer or his agents commits acts detrimental to honor and good reputation against the employees or their families; (vi) employer or his representatives offends the employees physically, except in case of self-defense; and (vii) employer reduces the employees' tasks in a way that affects their salaries.

Termination by Mutual Agreement

The Labor and Employment Reform implemented a new type of termination: termination by mutual agreement. The employment may be terminated by mutual agreement between the employee and the company, as established by Article 484-A of the Brazilian Labor Law, as amended by the Labor and Employment Reform, as per the terms agreed by the parties.

5.2. Mandatory Severance Payments

Termination Without Cause by the Company

Employees being terminated without cause are entitled to the following severance payments:

(a) salary balance due as from the last pay date up to the termination date (including base salary, bonus, commissions or variable compensation, etc.);
(b) indemnification for accrued and unused vacation (if any) equals to the employee's days of pending vacation multiplied by 1/30 of his/her monthly remuneration, plus a vacation bonus equals to 1/3 of such amount;
(c) accrued proportional vacation equals to 1/12 of the employee's monthly remuneration multiplied by the number of months (or fraction greater than fifteen days) worked since the last accrual period, plus a vacation bonus equals to 1/3 of such amount;
(d) proportional 13th salary equals to 1/12 of the employee's monthly remuneration multiplied by the number of months (or fraction greater than fifteen days) worked between the beginning of the calendar year and the termination date;
(e) indemnification for lack of prior notice[4] (if the employer decides that termination should be effective immediately) equals to thirty days of salary, plus three days per year of services rendered to the company up to sixty additional days, totaling ninety days; and
(f) Severance Guarantee Fund ("FGTS") termination fine equals to 50% of the balance of the employee's Severance Guarantee Fund (80% of such amount shall be paid to the employee and 20% to the Government). The balance of the employee's Severance Guarantee Fund is comprised by monthly deposits of 8% of the employee's monthly remuneration carried out by the employer during the employment relationship.

In addition to that, if the termination without cause is carried out up to thirty days before the date of the mandatory annual salary adjustment established by the relevant collective bargaining agreement,[5] the employer must pay a fine equals to one monthly salary of the employee.

---

4. Considering that the prior notice period is considered as a part of the employment agreement; it must be considered for the purpose of calculating the amounts related to the items (c) and (d) described above.
5. If the employer pays the prior notice in lieu, the respective period must be considered for this purpose.

Severance payments must be carried out within ten days as from the last day of work.

The relevant collective bargaining agreement may provide additional indemnities and benefits in case of termination.

The employer must observe the withholding income tax and social security charges levying on the severance payments.

Termination for Cause by the Company

In case the employee is terminated for cause, he/she will not be entitled to receive the payments established in the items 'c', 'd', 'e' and 'f' described above, but only those listed in the items 'a' and 'b', applicable in case of termination without cause.

Severance payments must be carried out within ten days as from the last day of work.

The relevant collective bargaining agreement may provide additional indemnities and benefits in case of termination.

The employer must observe the withholding income tax and social security charges levying on the severance payments.

Resignation by the Employee

In case the employee resigns from his/her position, he/she will not be entitled to receive the payments established in items 'e' and 'f' described above, but only those listed in items 'a', 'b', 'c' and 'd', applicable in case of termination without cause.

Severance payments must be carried out within ten days as from the last day of work.

The relevant collective bargaining agreement may provide additional indemnities and benefits in case of termination.

The employer must observe the withholding income tax and social security charges levying on the severance payments.

Constructive Termination

In case of a constructive termination, the employee will be entitled to receive the same payments that are due in case of termination without cause by the company.

Termination by Mutual Agreement

In case of termination by mutual agreement, the following severances are due: (1) in half: (i) prior notice, if paid in lieu; and (ii) FGTS termination fine; and (2) if in full: the remaining severance payments described in items 'a', 'b', 'c', 'd' above, applicable in case of termination without cause.

The employee will be able to withdraw 80% of the balance of his/her FGTS account. In this case, however, the employee will not be entitled to unemployment insurance.

Severance payments must be carried out within ten days as from the last day of work.

The relevant collective bargaining agreement may provide additional indemnities and benefits in case of termination.

The employer must observe the withholding income tax and social security charges levying on the severance payments.

5.3. Fines and Penalties

If the severance payments described above are not paid within the above-mentioned deadlines, the employee will be entitled to receive a fine equivalent to one monthly salary.

6. LAYOFFS, REDUCTIONS IN FORCE, AND/OR REDUNDANCIES AS A RESULT OF JOB ELIMINATIONS OR OTHER RESTRUCTURING

6.1. Overview

As of November 2017, Brazilian employment and labor laws expressly do not require the involvement of the labor union representing the employees to negotiate mass layoffs, reductions in workforce, redundancies or other kind of restructures. This is so because, according to Article 477–A of Brazilian Labor Law, as amended by the Labor and Employment Reform, individual; collective; and mass terminations shall be equally treated for all purposes, not being required a prior authorization of the labor union or the negotiation of a collective bargaining agreement. In any case, depending on the specific circumstances of the company and its business/operations, it may be recommendable to involve the employees' labor union in order to avoid potential strikes and future individual and/or collective lawsuits.

6.2. Voluntary Termination Program

As an alternative to mass layoffs, public and private companies commonly implement a Voluntary Termination Program. The Voluntary Termination

Program shall be negotiated with the relevant labor union in order to avoid future lawsuits regarding the validity of such program.

According to Article 477-B of Brazilian Labor Law, as amended by the Labor and Employment Reform, the Voluntary Termination Program, when established in a collective bargaining agreement, grants a full and irrevocable release of the rights that may arise from the employment relationship, unless otherwise expressly stipulated by the parties.

A Voluntary Termination Program establishes a severance package that includes the mandatory severance payments (Please refer to item 5.2) and additional benefits (e.g., extension of medical insurance after the termination), as well as the payment of an indemnification usually based on the length of time that the employee has worked for the company.

Finally, in order for the program to be considered valid before Brazilian labor courts, some legal requirements must be fulfilled. For example, employees have to have the option to participate or not in the program, the conditions of the program cannot be discriminatory, and the program has to provide a clear description of the benefits that will be granted to the employees.

6.3. Fines and Penalties

There are no fines or penalties imposed for mass layoffs, reductions in force, redundancies or any other type of restructure. However, if the severance payments due are not paid within the legal deadlines, general penalties will apply, as described in item 5.3.

7. LABOR AND EMPLOYMENT LAW IMPLICATIONS UPON ACQUISITION OR SALE OF A BUSINESS

7.1. Overview

According to Articles 10 and 448 of Brazilian Labor Law, changes in the ownership or in the legal structure of a company shall not affect the relationship maintained with its employees.

As a consequence, in accordance with Article 448–A of the Brazilian Labor Law, as amended by the Labor and Employment Reform, in cases of mergers, acquisitions, spin-offs, and/or substantial transfer and assignments of assets and/or goodwill, the successor (the buyer) will be considered as primarily liable for all labor and employment rights/benefits due to the employees of the succeeded company transferred to the buyer. Including, depending on how the transaction is structured, the buyer may be held liable for labor and employment rights/benefits due before the transaction (especially for those due to the employees who were transferred to the buyer). Moreover, in case of acquisition of the entire company, the buyer may even be liable for labor and employment rights/benefits due to employees that were terminated before the transaction.

On its turn, the succeeded company will remain liable for labor and employment rights/benefits due before the transaction to the employees transferred to the successor, but solely in a secondary manner and if the successor does not have means to grant/pay such rights/benefits and the transaction was implemented aiming solely at circumventing the application of Brazilian labor and employment laws or in case of fraud.

Moreover, in accordance with Article 448—A, sole paragraph, of the Brazilian Labor Law, as amended by the Labor and Employment Reform, in case of fraud, the succeeded company will remain jointly liable with the successor.

7.2. Acquired Rights

The change in the ownership or in the legal structure of a company shall not cause any harm to affected employees, meaning that at least the same salary and benefits must continue to be provided to them after the transaction. Therefore, the acquiring company cannot remove or cancel any benefit that used to be provided to them, regardless of any written agreement or settlement between the parties. However, this does not mean that the acquiring company is required to keep the exact same compensation package and benefits that used to be provided to them, meaning that, as long as it complies with certain rules, it may change their compensation package.

7.3. Acquisition and Sale Checklist

A due diligence is recommendable especially to analyze the employment and labor conditions of the employees of the company being acquired, the compensation package granted to them, their union representation, the existence of guarantees of employment, the existence of judicial and/or administrative lawsuits and/or procedures and other labor and employment liabilities that may directly affect the transaction and the interests of the acquiring company.

A complete analysis of the impacts of a merger between workforces of different companies is also highly recommendable in order to avoid future claims based on equal pay for equal work rules. The acquiring company should review salary levels and compensation structures currently granted to the employees of the company being acquired. In addition to that, the acquiring company must verify if the labor union representing the employees of the company being acquired will remain the same or will change after the transaction is closed in order to comply with the correct collective bargaining agreement and correctly collect union dues.

8. USE OF ALTERNATIVE WORKFORCE: INDEPENDENT CONTRACTORS, OUTSOURCING, AND TEMPORARY OR LEASED WORKERS

8.1. Overview

In some circumstances, companies may contract individuals: (i) as independent contractors to provide, for example, consulting services; (ii) through a third-party company to provide specific services, such as security and cleaning services; and (iii) as temporary or leased workers.

8.2. Independent Contractors

a. Definition

Independent contractors are individuals who have expertise in a specific field and carry out their services to the contracting company on an independent basis, without being subject to control of working hours or subordination before the contracting company's employees and representatives.

The main difference between an employee and an independent contractor is that the employee is subject to subordination and the independent contractor render services on an independent basis.

Thus, in case the independent contractor renders his/her services under the direction/subordination of the contracting company, an employment relationship may be pronounced between the independent contractor and the contracting company in case of a labor lawsuit or a labor inspection. In this case, the independent contractor will be entitled to receive all labor and employment benefits provided by Brazilian employment and labor laws and the collective bargaining agreement applicable to the employees of the contracting company.

b. Creating the Relationship

The relationship between the contracting company and the independent contractor should be regulated by a written services agreement addressing, at least, the services that will be rendered, the length of the relationship (starting date and term), the fees, and the duties of both parties.

c. Compensation Package

An independent contractor will not be entitled to "salary," benefits and other mandatory rights due to employees, but solely to the services fees established in the services agreement. In addition to that, it is not recommendable to provide to an independent contractor benefits that are usually provided to employees, such as health insurance, bonus payments, etc.

8.3. Outsourced Workers / Outsourcing of Activities

Up to March 31, 2017, there was no legal provision regarding outsourcing in Brazil. The subject was regulated solely by Precedent No. 331 issued by Brazilian Superior Labor Court, according to which solely the outsourcing of the contracting company's secondary activities would be lawful, i.e., the activities not related to its productive activities, such as security services, cleaning, IT, etc. On August 30, 2018, however, the Brazilian Supreme Court ruled that the outsourcing of main activities by companies is lawful.

In addition to that, according to such Precedent, even if the contracting company solely outsources its secondary activities, the employees and representatives of the contracting company cannot directly control the outsourced workers, under the penalty of an employment relationship being pronounced directly between them and the contracting company. The pronouncement of an employment relationship directly between the outsourced workers and the contracting company may occur in case of a labor lawsuit or a labor inspection.

In case an employment relationship is pronounced directly between the outsourced workers and the contracting company, they would be entitled to all benefits due to the regular employees of the contracting company, such as the benefits provided for in the collective bargaining agreement applicable to them. Moreover, the contracting company may be subject to the payment of administrative fines and collective damages for labor standards offenses, if any.

Finally, even if the outsourcing is considered lawful, Precedent No. 331 establishes that the contracting company may still be held secondarily liable for any labor obligation not complied with by the third-party company in relation to the outsourced workers.

On March 31, 2017, however, a new law (Law No. 13,429/2017) regulating outsourcing in Brazil was approved. On November 2017, this new law was later amended by the Labor and Employment Reform in order to establish that it would be possible for companies to outsource specific and determined services irrespectively of the main activities of the contractor including its core business.

In line with Precedent No. 331, Law No. 13,129/2017 also determines that the contracting company is liable on a secondary basis for any labor obligations not complied with by the contractor in relation to the outsourced workers.

Finally, it is also important to highlight that Law No. 13,429/2017 does not avoid the recognition of a direct employment between the outsourced workers and the contracting company in case the requirements of the employment relationship are found to exist.

8.4. Temporary Workers

The hiring of temporary workers is regulated by Law No. 6,019/1974, as amended by Law No. 13,429/2017, and Federal Executive Decree No. 73,841/1974. According to Law No. 6,019/1974, as amended by Law No. 13,429/2017, it is only possible to hire temporary workers through a manpower supplier company that has a special license granted by the Brazilian Labor and Employment Ministry with the sole purpose of: (a) replacing individuals on leave of absence (e.g., a pregnancy leave); or (b) meeting a complementary increase in services.

As a general rule, according to Law No. 6,019/1974, as amended by Law No. 13,429/2017, a temporary worker can render services to the same contracting company for up to 180 days, extendable for up to additional 90 days, in certain circumstances. At the end of this period, if the temporary worker continues to work for the same contracting company, he/she will be considered a regular employee of the contracting company.

Also, the contracting company may be held jointly and severally liable for labor and social security obligations related to temporary workers if: (a) the manpower supplier company goes bankrupt; and/or (b) such hiring is not in accordance with Law No. 6,019/1974 (if the hiring is pronounced to be unlawful, the contracting company may also be considered as the employer of such workers). In addition, according to case law, even if such hiring complies with Law No. 6,019/1974, the contracting company may still be held secondarily liable for all obligations related to the employment agreement between the supplier company and the temporary worker.

9. UNIONS AND COLLECTIVE BARGAINING

9.1. Overview of Unions Representation

Brazilian Federal Constitution establishes that employers and employees shall be represented by a union, in accordance with the employer's location and main activity, regardless of affiliation.

As a result, employers and employees have to comply with the provisions of the relevant collective bargaining agreement negotiated between their respective unions.

The employer is also responsible for withholding the employees' union dues and transferring the withheld amount to their union. As of November 2017, however, the withholding is only due when expressly authorized by the employee according to Article 579 of the Brazilian Labor Law, as amended by the Labor and Employment Reform.

Brazilian labor laws also establish that employees belonging to a specific professional category shall be represented by the union representing their specific category, regardless of their employers' main activity (e.g., engineers, drivers, secretaries). Those employees may be entitled to the benefits provided by the collective bargaining agreements executed by their specific union and their employer or the union representing their employer, and not to the benefits foreseen by the one applicable to the other regular employees working for their employer.

9.2. Right of Employees to Join Unions

Employees are free to join any union. Nevertheless, the only union that may interfere in the employees' employment is the one representing the employees' category or the one representing the employees of their employers, according to their employers' main activities and location.

9.3. How Employees Select Unions

Please refer to item 9.1. As a general rule, employees are represented by a union in accordance with the employer's location and main activity, regardless of affiliation. However, if the employee belongs to certain specific categories, he/she must be represented by the union representing the employees of such specific category (e.g., engineers, drivers, secretaries).

9.4. Preelection Campaigning

There are no specific rules for preelection campaigning in Brazil.

9.5. Unfair Labor Practices

According to Brazilian labor laws, employers cannot terminate employees without cause as from the moment they register as a candidate for a position in the board of the union. If the employee is elected, the guarantee of employment is extended for one year after he/she leaves the position.

Brazilian labor laws also guarantee to employees freedom to go on strike in order to defend economic and/or professional interests. However, according to Brazilian labor laws, in order for a strike to be considered lawful, it must fulfill some requirements, such as having been voted by the employees and initiated upon prior notice to the employer. In any case, employers cannot adopt means to compel employees to work and hinder the strike. In this sense, for example, employers cannot terminate employees while they are on strike.

9.6. Relocation of Work/Shutdown of Business

Unions have no legal right to be informed or consulted on relocation or shutdown of business.

9.7. Employee Internal Commission

As of November 2017, due to the Labor and Employment Reform, companies employing more than 200 employees must allow the establishment of a commission to represent its employees within the company.

The commission must be composed by: (a) three members, for companies employing between 200 and 3,000 employees; (b) five members, for companies employing between 3,001 and 5,000 employees; or (c) seven members, for companies employing more than 5,000 employees.

The employee internal commission will have the following duties: (i) to represent employees before the administration of the company; (ii) to improve the relationship between the company and its employees based on the principles of good faith and mutual respect; (iii) to promote dialogue and understanding within the work environment in order to prevent conflicts; (iv) to seek solutions to the conflicts arising from the employment relationship, in a fast and efficient way, aiming at the effective application of legal and contractual rules; (v) to ensure fair and impartial treatment of employees, preventing any form of discrimination based on sex, age, religion, political opinion or labor union activity; (vi) to analyze specific claims of employees; and (vii) to monitor the compliance with labor, employment and social security laws and the applicable collective bargaining agreement.

The election for the commission shall be called, with a minimum notice of thirty days, counting from the end of the previous term of office, by means of a notice that must be fixed in the company, with ample publicity.

An electoral commission shall be formed, composed by five employees (not candidates) for the organization and monitoring of the electoral process.

The company and the labor union are forbidden to interfere in the electoral process. All employees of the company may apply, except those with a fixed-term contract, a suspended contract or who have received termination notice.

The commission shall be formed by the most voted candidates, by secret ballot (vote by proxy is not allowed). Members of the commission shall take office on the first working day following the election or the end of the previous term. If there are not enough candidates, the internal commission may be formed with a lower number of members. If there is no registration of candidacies, a minute shall be draw up by the electoral commission and a new election organized within one year.

Documents relating to the electoral process shall be issued in two copies. Those documents shall remain under the custody of the employees and of the company for a period of five years, available for consultation by any interested worker, the Labor Ministry and the Labor Public Prosecutor's Office.

The term of office of the members of the commission will be of one year. Members cannot be candidates in the two subsequent periods.

The term of office of a member of the commission does not imply in the suspension or interruption of the employment contract. Thus, members of the commission shall remain in the exercise of their duties in the company.

From the registration of the candidature until one year after the end of the term of office, members of the commission cannot be terminated without cause, unless due to a disciplinary, technical, economic or financial reason.

The decisions of the commission must always be voted and defined by simple majority. The commission will have powers to define its internal rules, independently.

9.8. Collective Negotiations: Which Rights/Obligations Can Be Negotiated and Which Rights/Obligations Cannot

The Labor and Employment Reform establishes that some matters can be negotiated with the labor union through a collective bargaining agreement. The negotiations of these specific matters will prevail even over the law, provided that statutory rights protected by the Brazilian Federal Constitution and by the Brazilian Labor Law (specifically those listed in Article 611-B, included by the Labor and Employment Reform) are not violated.

Collective bargaining agreements will prevail over the law when, among others, they cover matters established in Article 611-A of the Brazilian Labor Law, as amended by the Labor and Employment Reform. Among these matters, we highlight: (a) working hours, observing constitutional limits; (b) annual bank of hours; (c) reduction of meal break from one hour to thirty minutes; (d) identification of the positions that are classified as positions of trust; (e) company's internal rules; (f) representation of workers in the workplace; (g) home office, on call regime and intermittent work; (h) productivity compensation, including tips and compensation for individual performance; (i) alternative systems to control employees' working hours; (j) premium incentives; and (m) participation in the company's profit or results.

On the other hand, companies and labor unions cannot execute collective bargaining agreements related to the suppression or reduction of the rights established by Article 611–B of the Brazilian Labor Law, as amended by the Labor and Employment Reform. Among those minimum rights, we highlight: (a) professional identification standards; (b) nominal value of the thirteenth salary; (c) compensation of night work superior than daytime work; (d) paid annual vacations plus vacation bonus; (e) maternity leave of ate least one hundred and twenty days; (f) paternity leave under the terms fixed by law; (g) protection of the labor market of woman, with specific incentives, according to the law; (h) additional remuneration for painful, unhealthy or dangerous activities; (i) retirement; (j) accident insurance at the expense of the employer; (k) right to strike; (l) freedom of professional or union association, including the right not to suffer, without previous consent, collections or salary discounts established by a collective bargaining agreement or collective convention; and (m) prohibition of discrimination in regard to compensation and admission criteria for disabled persons.

10. WORKING CONDITIONS: WORKING HOURS AND PAYMENT OF WAGES UNDER STATUTE OR COLLECTIVE BARGAINING AGREEMENTS

10.1. Overview

Brazilian Federal Constitution and Brazilian Labor Law limit the regular working hours to eight hours per day and forty-four hours per week. Although this is a general rule, employees subject to especial working conditions (e.g., employees working under uninterrupted fixed shifts, drivers, aeronauts, journalists, etc.) may be subject to different working hours and schedules.

In addition to that, Brazilian Federal Constitution sets forth that salaries cannot be lower than the minimum wage, which is nationally established and annually readjusted.

10.2. Minimum Wage

According to Article 7, item IV, of Brazilian Federal Constitution and Article 76 of Brazilian Labor Law, the minimum wage aims at meeting the basic needs of employees and their families. Brazilian Federal Constitution also establishes that, even if the employee receives variable remuneration, his/her monthly remuneration cannot be lower than the minimum wage.

Currently, the Brazilian national minimum wage is BRL 954 per month. This minimum wage is updated every year. Some Brazilian States, however, adopt higher minimum wages applicable solely in their territories, at their entire discretion.

Furthermore, collective bargaining agreements may determine specific minimum wages applicable solely for the employees subject to them. In this case, however, they cannot establish a minimum wage lower than the national or the relevant state minimum wage.

10.3. Overtime

According to Article 59 of Brazilian Labor Law, overtime cannot exceed two hours per day. In any case, if an employee ends up working more than two overtime hours in a given day, all overtime hours worked (even those beyond the two-hours limit) must be paid to him/her. In addition to that, overtime hours must be paid with an additional of at least: (i) 50% over the regular hourly wage, if the overtime is carried out on a regular working day; or (ii) 100% over the regular hourly wage, if the overtime is carried out on a rest day or a holiday. Collective bargaining agreements, however, may establish higher overtime premiums.

Provided that the employee agrees with it, it is possible to offset overtime hours worked in one day by working fewer hours in the following days within the same month. In this case, if all overtime hours are offset, no overtime pay will be due to the employee. If the company, however, intends to be able to offset overtime hours worked in one day by allowing the employee to work fewer hours in the following days within a period longer than a month, the company must execute a "bank of hours" policy, which is subject to specific requirements and may be executed through individual agreements (if valid for up to six months) or a specific collective bargaining agreement (if valid for more than six months and up to twelve months).

10.4. Meal and Rest Periods

Article 71 of Brazilian Labor Law establishes that: (i) employees working more than four hours and up to six hours per day are entitled to a meal break of fifteen minutes; and (ii) employees working more than six hours per day are entitled to a meal break of, at least, one hour, but no longer than two hours. Employees working less than four hours per day are not entitled to meal breaks. Meal breaks shall not be considered working hours, and, thus, are not paid.

In addition to that, according to Article 66 of Brazilian Labor Law, employees are entitled to, at least, eleven hours of rest between two working days and, furthermore, based on Law No. 605/1949, employees are entitled to a paid weekly rest day, preferably on Sundays.

10.5. Deductions from Wages

According to Brazilian Labor Law and case law, salary deductions are not allowed unless they are: (i) related to advance payment; (ii) legally allowed (such as the ones related to social security contributions and withholding income tax); (iii) foreseen by the relevant collective bargaining agreement; or (iv) in the benefit of the employee, provided that previously authorized by him/her.

Also, in case the employee causes any damage to the company, the company is allowed to carry out salary deductions in order to compensate such damages if they were intentionally caused or if such deduction is authorized by the employee, even if the damage was not intentional.

10.6. Garnishment

Wages may be seized by a judicial decision in case the employee is obliged, for example, to provide child support. Companies must always comply with judicial decisions in this regard.

10.7. Exemptions to Wage and Hour Laws

Brazilian Labor Law determines that employees performing activities/services outside the company's premises that are not compatible with a defined working schedule are not entitled to overtime payment, as long as this employment condition is specified in the employees' employment agreements and in the employees' Employment and Social Security Booklets.

Brazilian Labor Law also establishes that employees holding management positions, i.e., employees receiving remuneration at least 40% higher than their subordinates and holding powers to hire, fire and give orders to other employees, are also not entitled to overtime payments.

In addition, the Brazilian Labor Law establishes that employees who work in a home office regime are also exempt from the controlling of working hours, and, thus, are not entitled to overtime payments.

As of November 2017, due to the Labor and Employment Reform, home office is regulated in Brazil. For purposes of Brazilian Labor Law, home office is considered to be the provision of services predominantly rendered outside the employer's premises, with the use of information and communication technologies which, by their nature, do not constitute external work.

Eventual attendances at the employer's premises to perform specific activities that require the presence of the employee in the employer's establishment does not deprive the nature of the home office regime.

Home office must be expressly regulated in written. The equipment and infrastructure costs must be defined in the employment agreement. Employers shall also instruct employees on the precautions that need to be taken in order to avoid work-related accidents and diseases, and employees must sign a term undertaking to follow the instructions provided.

It is possible for the employee to change his/her home office regime to a conventional regime by means of an amendment to the employment contract.

The employer, by his own determination, may alter the employee's home office regime, provided that the employer observes a fifteen days adaptation period, regulated by an amendment to the employment contract.

However, in case these employees are subject to control of working hours, they will no longer be considered exempt employees and will be entitled to receive overtime pay.

10.8. Child Labor

According to Article 7, item XXXIII, of Brazilian Federal Constitution and Article 403 of Brazilian Labor Law, the minimum age to work is 16. However, as from 14 years old, work is allowed as apprentice. In this case, special duties and responsibilities may apply (e.g., special conditions of working periods, prohibition of certain work places or night work, etc.). In addition to that, employees under 18 years old cannot work under hazard and dangerous conditions.

10.9. Recordkeeping Requirements

a. Information and Documents That Must Be Maintained/Retained

As a general rule, labor- and employment-related documents (such as employment agreements, control of working hours, termination forms, etc.) must be maintained for, at least, five years during the employment relationship and for two years as from its termination.

In addition to that, depending on the type of the document, longer periods of maintenance may apply. As an example, payroll-related documents, medical certificates, work-accident communication forms, and social security-related documents must be maintained for ten years.

Furthermore, the Employee Registration Book (that describes the employees' personal information, such as name, date of birth, parental information, place of residency, hiring date, Social Security number, taxpayer registry number and identity card number, salary, vacation periods, promotions and special working conditions), the Book of Labor and Employment Inspections and the Daily Book must be maintained by companies for an undetermined period.

b. Failure to Maintain/Retain Required Records

In case of an inspection by labor authorities, if the company does not present a document requested by the relevant authority, administrative fines may be imposed for each document not presented and for each employee to which such documents are related.

10.10. Reductions in Compensation Caused by Economic Downturn

As a general rule, salaries are irreducible, and any amendments or modifications to the employment agreements previously agreed cannot be, directly or indirectly, detrimental to employees' interests, under the penalty of being considered null and void before courts.

As an exception, according to Brazilian Federal Constitution, salaries may be reduced by means of a collective negotiation between the company and the labor union representing its employees. As the salary is one of the most protected rights in Brazil, any reduction may only be considered lawful if negotiated with the relevant labor union and the company is able to evidence that it is facing financial and economical difficulties that justify the reduction of the employees' salaries.

Also, considering that salaries are paid in consideration to the work performed by the employees, it is common to collective negotiate the reduction of working hours along with salaries. In addition to that, the labor union may request the provision of other benefits in order to compensate the salary reduction. In this sense, for example, labor unions usually request the provision of guarantee of employment to the employees who will have their salaries reduced.

11. OTHER WORKING CONDITIONS AND BENEFITS: BY STATUTE, COLLECTIVE AGREEMENTS OR COMPANY POLICY

11.1. Health and Other Insurance

Social Security benefits in Brazil are provided primarily by the Brazilian Social Security Institute ("INSS"), which covers all employees and workers, including self-employed individuals.

The Brazilian Social Security System guarantees the contributors income in case of medical or sick leaves (work-related or not), maternity leave, permanent disabilities, retirement and death.

The Brazilian Social Security System is mainly regulated by the Brazilian Federal Constitution, Law No. 8,212/1991 and Law No. 8,213/1991.

Finally, there is also a public health system called *Sistema Único de Saúde (SUS)* provided by the Brazilian government to all citizens. However, considering its precarious conditions, companies usually provide a private health and life insurance for their employees.

11.2. Leaves of Absence

According to Brazilian employment and labor laws, employees are entitled to leaves in some specific situations. In addition to the provisions established by Brazilian employment and labor laws, collective bargaining agreements may foresee additional leaves to employees.

a. Bereavement Leave

Employees are entitled to two consecutive days of paid leave in case of death of relatives, such as spouse, ascendant, descendant, brothers and sisters, or any other person expressly declared in the employee's Employment and Social Security Booklet that lives under his/her economic dependency, as provided in Article 473, item I, of Brazilian Labor Law.

b. Marriage Leave

Employees are entitled to three working days of paid leave in case they get married, according to Article 473, item II, of Brazilian Labor Law.

c. Pregnancy Leave and Maternity Leave

Women are eligible for maternity leave, including when adopting a child. According to Article 392 of Brazilian Labor Law, women are entitled to a statutory paid maternity leave of 120 days, which is extendable for 180 days if the company complies with specific rules. The maternity leave may begin 28 days before the expected date of birth and the remaining period shall be taken after the birth of the child, depending of the doctor's decision.

d. Paternity Leave

Employees are entitled to five business days of paid leave as from the first business day following the birth of their child, according to Article 7 of Brazilian Federal Constitution and Article 10, first paragraph, of the Act of Transitional Constitutional Provisions ("ADCT"). The paternity leave may be extendable for twenty days if the company complies with specific rules.

e. Voter Registration Leave

Employees are entitled to up to two business days for purposes of voter registration, according to Article 473, item V, of Brazilian Labor Law.

f. Military Duty Leave

Employees are entitled to military duty leave for the period in which they need to comply with their military obligations, according to Article 473, item VI, of Brazilian Labor Law.

g. "SAT" Leave

Employees are entitled to SAT leave for the days in which they will take admission tests for college or university, according to Article 473, item VII, of Brazilian Labor Law.

h. Jury Duty Leave

Employees are entitled to jury duty leave for the period in which they need to comply with their civil obligations before courts, according to Article 473, item VIII, of Brazilian Labor Law.

i. Union Representative Duty Leave

If the employee is a union representative, he/she is entitled to a union representative duty leave whenever he/she has to attend an official meeting with any international organization in which Brazil is member, according to Article 473, item IX, of Brazilian Labor Law.

j. Medical or Sick Leave

Employees are entitled to go on sick leave whenever they present to their employer a medical certificate stating that they are not able to work due to an accident or illness (irrespectively if the accident or illness is work-related or not). In general, an accident/illness will be considered as "work-related" if the employee was injured while working/commuting or acquired an occupational disease/illness.

According to Brazilian laws, employers are responsible to pay to the employee his/her entire salary during the first fifteen days of sick leave (regardless of being work-related or not). After the first fifteen days of sick leave, the Brazilian Social Security Institute will be the responsible to pay a sick leave benefit to the employee, which is equal to 91% of the employee's contribution salary, as set forth in Article 61 of Law No. 8,213/1991.

The payment of this benefit begins on the sixteenth day of the employee's leave and lasts until he/she is: (i) declared fit for duty; or (ii) declared permanently disabled. If it is a nonwork-related sick leave, the employer will not be required to carry out FGTS deposits while the employee is on leave, based on Article 15, 6th paragraph, of Law No. 8,036/1990. However, if it is a work-related sick leave, the employer is required to continue carrying out FGTS deposits while the employee is on a work-related sick leave, based on Article 1, 5th paragraph, of Law No. 8,036/1990.

k. Leave to Attend Medical Appointments of Pregnant Spouses and Partners

Employees are entitled to up to two days to attend medical appointments and follow-up examinations during the period of pregnancy of their spouses or partners, according to Article 473, item X, of Brazilian Labor Law.

l. Child Care Leave

Employees are entitled to one day per year to accompany their child up to six years old to medical appointments, according to Article 473, item XI, of Brazilian Labor Law.

12. COMPANY'S OBLIGATION TO PROVIDE A SAFE AND HEALTHY WORKPLACE

12.1. Overview of Health and Safety in the Workplace and Environmental Laws and Regulations

Brazilian Federal Constitution guarantees to all workers protection against risks in the workplace. Rules concerning safety, health and hygiene in the workplace are further regulated mainly by Brazilian Labor Law and Normative Rules issued by the Labor and Employment Ministry.

According to such rules, companies cannot start their activities without a previous inspection carried out by the competent authorities (which must be repeated if there is any modification in the structure of the company's facilities). Also, depending on the risks related to the activities of the company based on a risk table issued by the Brazilian Labor and

Employment Ministry, companies will be obliged to have commissions specialized on health and safety in the workplace.

Companies are also required to have: (i) an Environmental Risk Prevention Program, under the rules established by Normative Rule No. 9 issued by the Labor and Employment Ministry; (ii) an Occupational Health and Medical Control Program, according to the rules established by Normative Rule No. 7 issued by the Labor and Employment Ministry; (iii) a Work Environmental Conditions Technical Report, under the rules set forth by Normative Rules Nos. 7 and 9; and (iv) an Ergonomic Report, under the terms established by Normative Rule No. 17 issued by the Labor and Employment Ministry. These programs and reports intend to identify, measure, and control risks within the workplace, and suggest preventive or corrective measures to be adopted by companies.

12.2. Rights of Employees

As described above, companies must comply with safety and health rules set forth by Brazilian Labor Law and Normative Regulations issued by the Brazilian Labor and Employment Ministry.

As a consequence, companies must adopt all measures necessary to assure a safe and healthy workplace. Specifically, companies must: (i) provide adequate and up to date training on health and safety at work to their employees; (ii) enforce the compliance with health and safety procedures; (iii) supervise the correct use of protection equipment by their employees; and (iv) carefully select employees who will be responsible for the activities to be performed, considering their specific professional expertise and background. Noncompliance with health and safety rules may provide grounds for constructive termination claims by employees against their employers.

Employees who carry out activities under unhealthy conditions (e.g., excessive heat or noise) must receive, on a monthly basis, a supplementary allowance equal to 10%, 20% or 40% over the minimum salary, depending on the level of the employee's exposure to the unhealthy condition.

In case employees carry out their activities under dangerous conditions (e.g., working with inflammables or explosives), they are entitled to receive a supplementary allowance corresponding to 30% over their monthly base salary. From a strictly technical standpoint, the supplementary allowances due to work under unhealthy and dangerous conditions cannot coexist. In case an employee works under both unhealthy and dangerous conditions, the company must pay the more beneficial supplementary allowance.

Finally, employees have the legitimate right to refuse any task or activity for which they are not duly trained or which may put them in obvious risk of injuries.

12.3. Rights of Employers

Employers have the right to enforce the laws, regulations and policies related to health and safety in the workplace. If an employee fails to comply with them, he/she may be subject to disciplinary measures up to the termination for cause.

12.4. Specific Standards

Depending on the company's business or the activities carried out by its employees (especially the level of risk related to such activities), there are specific standards for clothing, security equipment and measures. The majority of the security standards are not established by laws, but rather by Normative Rules issued by the Brazilian Labor and Employment Ministry.

In addition, companies may establish through internal policies additional standards of conduct deemed appropriate and necessary for the maintenance of a healthy and safe workplace.

12.5. Injury or Accident at Work

According to Articles 19–21 of Law No. 8,213/1991, "work-related accident" comprehends: (a) any accident triggered by the work carried out by the employee on behalf of the employer, causing the employee's death, or the permanent or temporary reduction or loss of the employee's work capacity; (b) any occupational disease (any illness that affects the employee due to the activities carried out by the employee on behalf of the employer); (c) any accident occurred during working hours in the workplace as a consequence of aggression; sabotage; terrorism; physical aggression; a third party or co-worker imprudence, negligence and inability; flood, fire, or any other unpredictable event; (d) an accidental contamination of the employee due to the work performed; and (e) any accident suffered by the employee while commuting from home to work and vice versa.

Any work-related accident, regardless of its severity, must be reported to the Social Security through a form called Work Accident Report (*Comunicado de Acidente do Trabalho*– CAT).

Due to a work-related accident or illness, employees may be entitled to a sick leave. Also, employees may file lawsuits claiming for compensation for moral and material damages that may arise from a work-related accident. To prevail in such lawsuit, the employee has to evidence a connection between the accident and the services, and the employer's negligence or deceitfulness.

12.6. WORKPLACE VIOLENCE

Companies are obliged to guarantee a workplace free of violence. Violence in the workplace may be either physical or psychological. While physical violence is not often seen, psychological violence may assume various forms, such as sexual or moral harassment.

Psychological violence is not easily identified and controlled and, therefore, employees, especially those holding management positions, shall be trained and instructed not only to identify improper behaviors, but also to know how to deal with these situations.

Generally, moral harassment is defined as a repeated or systematic intentional act carried out by superiors or co-workers tending to undermine the dignity or the integrity of the employee, exposing him/her to unpleasant, humiliating, bothering or vexatious situations, usually culminating in the termination of the employment relationship (since in such cases the relationship between the employee and the employer is undermined in such a way that the maintenance of the employment agreement is no longer possible). However, the termination is not essential. It is important to note that simple discomfort or annoyance is not sufficient to characterize moral harassment.

On its turn, sexual harassment may be defined as the constraint of someone in order to gain sexual advantage or favor, relying the offender on his/her status of supervisor or his/her influence over the victim, inherent to their employment status. For employment purposes, sexual harassment may be configured if the constraint is carried out: (i) without the victim's consent; (ii) by his/her superior and in exchange for or promise of favoritism or advantage; and (iii) in the context of an employment/contractual relationship.

Sometimes it is difficult to prove moral damages, as sadness, depression, feelings of humiliation are subjective feelings, but the judge will consider how a normal human being would feel if subject to the acts of the offender. The proof is most of the times made through witnesses, but e-mails, reports or any other written document may evidence the moral or sexual harassment. In addition to the negative impacts on employees as mentioned above, employers may be held liable for the payment of compensation for moral damages to the employee, and collective damages may be claimed by the Brazilian Public Labor Prosecutor's Office and the relevant labor union through class actions.

The legal basis for a claim of compensation for moral damages filed by employees against their employers is Article 5, items V and X, of Brazilian Federal Constitution, which establish that the individual's honor, image and privacy are inviolable and those who, by negligence or fraud, violate such rights must compensate the damage. To analyze a claim of compensation for moral damages due to moral or sexual harassment, Brazilian labor courts verify the existence of: (i) damage; (ii) an intentional act or omission of the offender; and (iii) the relationship of cause and effect between the damage and the intentional act or omission of the offender.

12.7. Fines and Penalties

Failure to comply with obligations related to health and safety in the workplace may trigger the imposition of fines by Brazilian labor authorities. Such fines vary depending on the violation, its seriousness and the number of employees affected. In the worst case scenario, whenever the conditions in the workplace are very harmful or the risk to the employee's physical integrity is very serious, the company's facilities may be shut down until the problems identified are solved. Moreover, in case of accidents at work, employees may file labor lawsuits claiming for compensation for damages. Historically, the amount of damages awarded by Brazilian labor courts to plaintiffs takes into consideration the seriousness of the offense, the impact on the employee's physical or psychological health, the employer's economic capacity and previous history of violations.

13. IMMIGRATION, SECONDMENT AND FOREIGN ASSIGNMENT

13.1. Hiring Foreigners to Work in Brazil

The engagement of foreigners is regulated by Law No. 13,445/2017 ("Immigration Law"), which foresees different types of visas and different rules applicable to foreigners, including foreign employees and statutory offices. Depending on the legal nature of the relationship, different rules and requirements may apply for the request and issuance of work visas.

13.2. Recruiting, Screening and Hiring Process

To hire a foreigner as an employee in Brazil, it is necessary to check if the foreigner is allowed to work in Brazil, as he/she may not be hired without the appropriate work permit/visa.

If the foreign is a legal resident in Brazil who is also allowed to work, the recruiting and hiring process is the same applicable to Brazilian employees. Most commonly, Brazilian companies recruit foreigners already working for a foreign company belonging to its economic group.

In order to obtain a work permit for a foreign employee, the company has to comply with requirements established by the Brazilian Labor and Employment Ministry.

Employers should be aware that some benefits granted to expatriates (such as a house allowance, school fees for children, among others) may be deemed as salary for the purposes of calculating and collecting labor and employment charges and social security contributions.

13.3. Obligation of Employer to Enforce Immigration Laws

Employers may not employ foreigners without the appropriate work permits. It is a breach not only of immigration laws, but also of employment laws, since the company is not able to hire foreigners as proper employees. Employees without authorization may be forced to leave Brazil.

13.4. Fines and Penalties

Hiring foreigners without work permits may subject the Brazilian company to pay administrative fines to labor, immigration and social security authorities, since without a work permit the employer is not able to establish a regular employment agreement and pay all labor, employment and social security obligations due under Brazilian laws. Additionally, authorities may warn the Brazilian Public Labor Prosecutor's Office to start an investigation against the company.

13.5. Secondment/Foreign Assignment

Brazilian employees under temporary working assignments abroad are subject to the protection of Brazilian employment laws when they are more favorable than the laws of the place of the working assignment.

Employers shall pay for the transfer costs, and the employee may be entitled to the benefits provided for in the relevant collective bargaining agreement.

In any case, depending on the characteristics of the working assignment (e.g., temporary or permanent) specific rules may apply.

14. RESTRICTIVE COVENANTS AND PROTECTION OF TRADE SECRETS AND CONFIDENTIAL INFORMATION

14.1. Overview

Brazilian Labor Law establishes that an employment agreement may be terminated for cause if the employee: (i) performs negotiations, by himself/herself or through third parties competing with his/her employer; and/or (ii) violates the company's trade secrets. Employers may also be entitled to claim compensation for damages. Specifically regarding post-termination obligations, many companies in Brazil execute both employment and termination agreements with restrictive covenants, such as noncompete, nondisparagement and nonsolicitation obligations.

14.2. Trade Secrets

In Brazil, confidential information has statutory protection. According to Brazilian Penal Code, it is a criminal offense to disclose a secret known as a result of the provision of services.

In addition to that, Brazilian Intellectual Property Law establishes that it is a criminal offense to disclose trade secrets and other relevant commercial information known as a result of the provision of services or to use confidential information acquired through illegal means, without the relevant owner's consent. Finally, as described above, Article 482 of Brazilian Labor Law also establishes that the disclosure of confidential information/trade secrets is cause for termination.

In order to clarify what is actually deemed a trade secret, employment agreements often include broad definitions of confidential information. Usually, employers also include termination procedures to protect trade secrets, such as obligations to return the company's property upon the company's request or the termination of the employment relationship.

14.3. Restrictive Covenants: Noncompete and Nonsolicitation

As described above, employees have a noncompetition obligation while they are employed. However, after termination, although employees are still prohibited from engaging in any unfair competition against their former employer, there are no specific laws imposing post-termination obligations and/or restrictive covenants, such as noncompete or nonsolicitation obligations.

Regarding noncompete obligations, Brazilian labor judges have some restrictions in accepting noncompete obligations enforceable after the termination of the employment as they consider that this type of obligation would limit the individual's right of employment. In view of that, it is highly recommendable to: (i) establish this obligation solely to key employees; (ii) limit the extent of the noncompete obligation (both geographically and regarding the competitor definition); and (iii) establish a compensation for such obligation to be paid by the company (proportional to the period of noncompete, that cannot exceed two years, and the extension of obligation).

Finally, regarding nonsolicitation obligations, according to Brazilian case law, although nonsolicitation obligations enforceable after termination are acceptable, they may be difficult to be enforced as they are easy to be circumvent and employees may always apply for jobs themselves and customers and suppliers may voluntarily procure business with a former employee.

15. PROTECTION OF WHISTLEBLOWING CLAIMS

15.1. Overview

There are no legal provisions in Brazil related to whistleblowing. However, companies may, at their entire discretion, establish provisions in this regard in their internal policies/rules.

16. PROHIBITION OF DISCRIMINATION IN THE WORKPLACE

16.1. Overview of Antidiscrimination Laws

Brazilian Federal Constitution and Brazilian employment and labor laws prohibit differences in salary, job functions and hiring procedures based on gender, age, color, race, religion or marital status, as well as to any distinction due to the type of work performed by employees (manual, technical or intellectual work) or among the respective professionals.

Specifically, Law No. 9,029/1995 establishes that companies cannot adopt discriminatory practices aiming at obstacle the access to, or the maintenance of, an employment relationship based on gender, origin, race, color, marital status, familiar situation or age. In addition to that, companies cannot subject women to pregnancy or sterilization tests.

Convention No. 111 issued by the International Labor Organization (ILO) (which is ratified by the Brazilian government) establishes basic rules on discrimination in the workplace.

Under the Convention, discrimination is defined as every distinction, exclusion, or preference based on race, color, sex, religion, political opinion, nationality, or place of origin that may result in the annulment or reduction of equal opportunities or treatment in a workplace or profession.

According to it, discriminatory acts do not include the definition of specific skills for a job (such as graduation, language, professional experience, etc.), as well as any measure that may affect a person suspect of involvement or practice of prejudicial activities to the public security, reserved his/her right to defend him/herself against such acts. Also, special provisions for protection or assistance foreseen in other ILO Conventions are not considered as discriminatory acts either.

In case of discrimination in the workplace, employers may be subject to administrative fines, prohibition to obtain loans or finance from official financial institutions, individual lawsuits filed by employees or candidates claiming for compensation for moral damages and class actions.

16.2. Age Discrimination

Based on Article 461 of Brazilian Labor Law, employers cannot discriminate based on age.

Apart from that, there is no specific law prohibiting age discrimination, especially regarding elderly workers. Despite of that, any candidate not hired solely due to his/her age may file a lawsuit against the company pleading for the payment of compensation for moral damages.

16.3. Race Discrimination

According to Brazilian Federal Constitution, discriminatory acts infringing fundamental freedom and rights are prohibited. Specifically, race discrimination is a federal felony that cannot be put up on bail.

Prison sentences can be imposed in case of conviction for race discrimination. In addition to that, any candidate who was not hired solely due to his/her race may file a lawsuit against the company pleading for the payment of compensation for moral damages.

16.4. Sex Discrimination

As described above, Brazilian Labor Law requires equal pay for equal work, regardless of the gender of the employee. Any candidate who was not hired solely due to his/her sex may file a lawsuit against the company pleading for the payment of compensation for moral damages.

16.5. Disability Discrimination

Brazilian Federal Constitution prohibits discrimination against disabled employees. In addition to that, Law No. 10,098/2000 establishes rules for the accessibility of disabled employees.

Furthermore, according to Law No. 8,213/1991, companies employing one hundred or more employees must guarantee between 2% and 5% of their positions to employees with disabilities, depending on the number of employees. Furthermore, if a company terminates an employee with disability, it will have to hire another one to comply with such rule. In case of noncompliance, a fine may be imposed for each disabled employee that should have been hired. However, before imposing such fine, the Brazilian Labor Public Prosecutor's Office often investigates the company in order to verify the reasons for such noncompliance. Companies may enter into an Agreement for Adjustment of Conduct with the Labor Public Prosecutor's Office under which the company commits to comply with the legal minimum quota within a certain deadline to avoid the fine.

16.6. National Origin Discrimination

National origin discrimination is prohibited by the aforementioned ILO Convention.

16.7. Religious Discrimination

Religious discrimination is prohibited by the aforementioned ILO Convention.

16.8. Military Services Discrimination

Under Brazilian Labor Law, the absence of an employee on account of the exigencies of military service or any other public duty shall not be a ground for the employment termination.

However, employees are not entitled to return to the position he/she used to hold before being absent due to military services unless he/she notifies the employer of his/her intention to return within thirty days from the date of discharge from the military services or termination of the public duty, by means of a telegram or registered letter. Moreover, during the first ninety days of absence, the employee absent due to the military service must continue to receive his/her salary.

16.9. Pregnancy Discrimination

According to Law No. 9,029/1995, companies cannot subject women to pregnancy or sterilization tests and discriminate against pregnant women.

Furthermore, Brazilian Federal Constitution provides to pregnant women guarantee of employment as from the moment of the discovery of the pregnancy up to five months after the child's birth.

16.10. Marital Status Discrimination

Discrimination due to marital status is prohibited by Law No. 9,029/1995.

16.11. Sexual Orientation Discrimination

Sexual orientation is not expressly protected under Brazilian law. However, based on general principles of law, companies cannot discriminate based on sexual orientation.

16.12. Retaliation

Companies are not allowed to retaliate against an employee who filed a labor lawsuit against the company claiming for compensation for moral damages arising from discrimination or complained against an employee who discriminated him/her in the workplace.

16.13. Constructive Termination

Based on Article 483 of Brazilian Labor Law, an employee may consider his/her employment terminated and claim before courts the appropriate compensation in case he/she is discriminated.

The employee who alleges the constructive termination will have to evidence before courts that he/she indeed was discriminated in the workplace. By proving such discrimination, the employee will be entitled to receive all severance payments due as if he/she was terminated without cause.

17. SMOKING IN THE WORKPLACE

17.1. Overview

There are no legal provisions in Brazil related to smoking in workplace. However, according to the Decree No. 8,262/2014, it is illegal to smoke in inside private or public spaces in Brazil.

18. USE OF DRUGS AND ALCOHOL IN THE WORKPLACE

18.1. Overview

Employees may be terminated for cause for habitual or work-related inebriety as determinate by Article 482 of Brazilian Labor Law. Termination may occur when the worker is not capable, due to the inebriety to perform his/her job related activities. In making this determination, courts and scholars consider a number of factors, including the length of service of the employee, the frequency of such conduct, the intention of the employee and his/her resistance to alcohol.

Regarding the use of drugs in the work-place, although there is no legal provision on this matter, companies may terminate employees caught using or possessing drugs within the company's facilities or during the working hours, even if outside the company's facilities, for cause.

Employers are not allowed to subject employees to alcohol or drug tests, and such tests shall not be considered as condition for the hiring of an employee, unless the performance of his/her activities under the effect of alcohol/drugs may put his/her life or the lives of others in danger.

According to Brazilian case law, before deciding to terminate the employee, employers shall carefully deal these situations and encourage the treatment of alcoholism/drug use, as alcoholism and drug use are medical problems. In fact, Brazilian labor courts understand that alcoholism is an illness and alcohol consumption by addicts should no longer be used as a basis for disciplinary actions or termination for cause. That said, if the employer verifies that one of its employees is addicted to alcohol, he/she should not be punished or terminated for cause, but rather referred for treatment to the social security authorities. Employers may also require employees to attend lectures or training courses on drug and alcohol dependence. In addition to that, internal policies may be drafted by companies in this regard, indicating the application of penalties in case any employee use drugs or alcohol within the company or during the performance of his/her activities.

19. AIDS, HIV, SARS, BLOODBORNE PATHOGENS

19.1. Overview

Employees affected by AIDS, HIV, SARS and other blood borne pathogens are not entitled to guarantee of employment and, in this sense, from a technical standpoint, there is no legal obstacle for the employer to terminate the employment agreement. However, the employer may not require blood exams from employment candidates related to such diseases as a condition for their admission. In case blood tests for this purpose are required, it may be considered as discrimination against employees. Recently, the Superior Labor Court has taken the position that the termination of employment of employees with such diseases is presumed to be motivated by discrimination. In this sense, when terminating the employment agreement of employees affected by these kinds of diseases, employers have to be prepared to evidence that the termination was motivated by reasons unrelated to the disease, such as due to economic, financial, or performance reasons in case the employee decides to challenge his termination before courts.

20. DRESS REQUIREMENTS

20.1. Overview

Employers may impose dress and grooming requirements in their internal policies. However, if uniforms are mandatory, employers shall provide them to the employees free of charges/costs. Employers may also include in the uniform the logos of the company or of partnership's companies and other identification items related to the activity rendered, as established in Article 456–A of the Brazilian Labor Law, as amended by the Labor and Employment Reform.

The cleaning of the uniform is the employee's responsibility, except in cases in which the procedures or products are different from those used for the hygiene of the usual uniforms.

21. PRIVACY, TECHNOLOGY AND TRANSFER OF PERSONAL DATA

21.1. Privacy Rights of Employees

Privacy rights are guaranteed by Article 5, item X, of Brazilian Federal Constitution.

As a general rule, sharing employees' data between companies belonging to the same economic group, when the reasons for that transfer are related to the companies' business (e.g., operational efficiency in the administration of employment relationships or compliance with legal obligations), would not be considered a privacy violation. However, if the employer intends to share employees' data for purposes other than general employment administration, the employer shall obtain a previous consent from employees in order to avoid any privacy violation claims.

Brazilian labor courts understand that corporate e-mails are a working tool, especially due to the fact that the employer may be deemed liable for the e-mails content. Thus, courts have maintained terminations for cause when employees share e-mails with inappropriate content (e.g., e-mails with pornographic material). However, as most decisions are based on the fact that employers have specific policies to address the use of e-mails and Internet, a written policy in this regard is recommendable. The same principle applies to tracking employees' access to websites in working computers.

Finally, surveillance devices (e.g., cameras) are also allowed for security purposes, but private places like toilets and changing rooms cannot be monitored by video.

22. WORKPLACE INVESTIGATIONS FOR COMPLAINTS OF DISCRIMINATION, HARASSMENT, FRAUD, THEFT, AND WHISTLEBLOWING

22.1. Overview

Workplace investigations may be conducted by the employer as a mechanism of control of a safe and fair work environment, as well as for the protection of its business, operations, and property. However, considering the employees' right to privacy and honor, every investigation process shall be carried out by the employer in a very discreet and respectful manner.

The investigation process has to be kept confidential by the company, as well as the reason for the investigation. Only the 'must know' employees shall be aware of the circumstances surrounding the investigation. Additionally, the company must assure that the employees who were involved in the investigation process are aware that the matter shall be treated as confidential.

As per the understanding of Brazilian labor courts, employees under investigation shall be granted with the right to know the allegations that triggered the investigation, and also shall be granted with the right to explain the specific facts and circumstances. Finally, it is important for companies to define the procedures that must be followed in an investigation as a way of assuring that all employees will be subject to equivalent treatment and disciplinary measures.

Internal investigations in the workplace must observe the following main principles:

Confidentiality: Companies must guarantee confidentiality to whistle-blowers, to employees under investigation (subjects) and employees that may become part of the investigation as witnesses. Only "must-know" individuals shall be aware of/have access to the internal investigation.

Intimacy/Privacy: Employees (including those under investigation) are not obliged to answer any question. Employers cannot force employees to provide any information. Employees, witnesses, whistle-blowers and subjects are not obliged to testify under oath before or out of courts.

Nonretaliation: Companies must guarantee that there will be no retaliation against whistle-blowers and/or witnesses.

Proportionality: Investigation procedures should be proportional to the potential violation under investigation. As a general rule, investigations are not subject to any formal/defined procedures.

For labor and employment purposes, all findings shall be filed and the company shall issue a final report regarding the investigation in order to present before courts if the subject end up being terminated for cause and later files a labor lawsuit against the company claiming that he/she was wrongfully terminated for cause. This is recommendable because it is the company's burden to evidence the occurrence of the violation/misconduct.

23. AFFIRMATIVE ACTION / NONDISCRIMINATION REQUIREMENTS

23.1. Overview

Affirmative actions are required for people with disabilities. Please refer to item 16.5.

24. RESOLUTION OF LABOR, DISCRIMINATION AND EMPLOYMENT DISPUTES: LITIGATION, ARBITRATION, MEDIATION AND CONCILIATION

24.1. Internal Dispute Resolution Process

In Brazil, it is not very common for employers to set up processes to resolve internal disputes, especially because Brazilian employment and labor laws are very protective towards employees, and it is not legally possible to obtain an out-of-court final and general release from employees.

24.2. Arbitration and Out-of-Court Releases

As a general rule, arbitration procedures are not binding between the parties of an employment relationship. Labor and employment-related disputes may always be subject before Brazilian labor courts by employees.

However, as of November 2017, the Labor and Employment Reform allows employees who hold a higher education degree and receive a monthly salary equal or greater than two times the maximum benefit paid by the National Social Security Institute (currently, this amount is equal to BRL 11,291.60[6]) to have autonomy to sign arbitration clauses to settle disputes. In this case, the arbitration clause will be binding.

As a general rule, out-of-court general releases are not enforceable before courts. This is so because Brazilian labor courts understand that, as labor and employment rights cannot be waived by employees.

However, as of November 2017, employees and employers may settle disputes through an out-of-court settlement, and, later, request the

6. This amount is valid for 2018 and may increase every year.

ratification of the out-of-court settlement before Brazilian Labor Courts. In this case, if the out-of-court settlement is ratified by Labor Courts and if the parties agreed to a general release, this general release will be binding.

24.3. Litigation

According to Article 114 of Brazilian Federal Constitution, Brazilian labor courts have jurisdiction over all work-related claims. Matters related to work and employment include claims from employees, sales agents and services providers, union disputes, moral and material damages claims due to work-related accidents or any other claims arising from a labor and/or employment relationship.

a. Brazilian Labor Courts Structure

There are three levels of labor courts:

- Lower Labor Courts.
- Regional Labor Courts (Court of Appeals).
- Superior Labor Court (Superior Court of Appeals).

b. Enforceability of Judgments

After entry of the first judgment in favor of the plaintiff, the judge will require an expert to calculate the amount owed to the plaintiff. The amount owed to the plaintiff will be subject to interest and monetary adjustments. Such amount will be deposited in a court bank account and the plaintiff will be able to withdraw the total amount after the issuance of a final decision, if in his/her favor. On the contrary, the defendant will be able to withdraw the deposited amount.

c. Appeal Standards

In order to appeal, defendants are legally required to pay a deposit to the court to guarantee the execution of the decision and the court fees. The deposit amount may vary according to the court that the party is appealing to. Note that this deposit is not applicable for plaintiffs and the deposit amount may be withdrawn by the party that deposited it if the labor claim is deemed groundless, or subtracted from the amount due to the plaintiff if the defendant is partially convicted.

d. Issues of Court Bias

Brazilian labor courts are an independent part of the Brazilian judicial system and are not subject to any political influence. Foreign and national companies have equal rights in court proceedings.

Labor judges shall analyze the labor lawsuit in accordance with the applicable laws, and shall pronounce the judgment at their own conviction, without any bound to any of the parties.

24.4. Fines, Penalties and Damages

Judges may decide to impose fines and penalties on employers and employees if one of the parties is litigating in bad faith. The amounts imposed may vary according to their conviction.

25. EMPLOYER RECORDKEEPING. DATA PROTECTION AND EMPLOYEE ACCESS TO PERSONNEL FILES AND RECORDS

25.1. Overview

Currently, there is no specific data protection law in force concerning employees in Brazil, except for the general rules set forth by Article 5, item X, of Brazilian Federal Constitution, that gives individuals rights to privacy and protection of their self-image. Therefore, it is necessary to establish a balance between employees' privacy and employer's use of the employee's information.

Thus, employers may use employees' information for administrative purposes only, and provided that using or sharing such information does not violate the employee's privacy rights.

It is also important to determine if the personal data that will be used by the company is, in fact, private data. Several relevant information may be in fact publicly or voluntarily disclosed by the employees (e.g., their e-mail address and/or office telephone numbers). In these cases, such information is not equivalent to personal secrets connected directly with the relevant person's intimacy. The protection granted to such publicly disclosed information is not as strong as the protection granted to nonpublicly disclosed information.

In this context, it is important to mention that, on August 15, 2018, Law No. 13,709/18, the "Personal Data Protection Law" that establishes rules for the protection of personal data, was sanctioned by the Brazilian President.

The Personal Data Protection Law was inspired by the General Data Protection Regulation (GDPR) and will enter into force eighteen months after its official publication, i.e., on February 15, 2020. Up to this date, companies doing business in Brazil need to adjust their internal practices in order to be in compliance with the new rules implemented by Law No. 13,709/18.

25.2. Personnel Files

Considering that there are no specific legal provisions regarding what constitutes personal/private records of employees, employers shall be cautious not to violate any privacy rules.

Brazilian labor courts, however, understand that corporate e-mail addresses and data records of the employees belong to the employer. As a result, employers shall analyze the kind of information that may need to be disclosed on a case-by-case basis.

25.3. Confidentiality Rules

Companies shall ensure that information provided by employees is used for administrative purposes only, and shall not be disclosed to third parties for any other reason. A company is deemed liable for acts performed by its employees in relation to employees' activities. Thus, if a human resources employee discloses confidential employee information (e.g., a medical condition), the employer may be liable for any damages caused due to such disclosure.

25.4. Employee Access

Employees may seek to have access to their information held by the company, and also to rectify or update their information.

26. REQUIRED NOTICES AND POSTINGS

26.1. Overview

According to Brazilian employment and labor laws, there are some documents and information that must be disclosed to the employees, such as: (i) working-hour schedules, especially when the employees work on shifts;

(ii) copy of the relevant collective bargaining agreement; (iii) notice of collective vacation; and (iv) information related to safety and health in the workplace, especially to advise the existence of hazardous and/or unhealthy conditions in the workplace.

Company's policies may also be disclosed in the notice board or in the company's intranet.

Such documents and information can be posted on a notice board in a visible place, so that the employees can have access to them. In case of nondisclosure of these documents and information, or the disclosure in a place of difficult access, labor authorities may notify the company to place the information in a visible and accessible location within the company.

www.ingramcontent.com/pod-product-compliance
Ingram Content Group UK Ltd.
Pitfield, Milton Keynes, MK11 3LW, UK
UKHW020151290926
15471UKWH00004B/819

9 789403 503905